Specs For
T-Rex

Maverick
Early Readers

'Specs For T-Rex'
An original concept by Jenny Jinks
© Jenny Jinks

Illustrated by Lucy Makuc

Published by MAVERICK ARTS PUBLISHING LTD

Studio 11, City Business Centre, 6 Brighton Road,

Horsham, West Sussex, RH13 5BB

© Maverick Arts Publishing Limited February 2020

+44 (0)1403 256941

A CIP catalogue record for this book is available at the British Library.

ISBN 978-1-84886-660-7

www.maverickbooks.co.uk

Blue

This book is rated as: Blue Band (Guided Reading)
This story is mostly decodable at Letters and Sounds Phase 4.
Up to five non-decodable story words are included.

Specs For T-Rex

by **Jenny Jinks**

illustrated by
Lucy Makuc

Steg was playing in his den.

"Can I play?" said Rex.

He did not see the log.

Ted was playing ball.

"Can I play?" said Rex.

Rex did not see the ball. *POP!*

Rex!

Dips was playing hide and seek.

"Can I play?" said Rex.

But Rex did not see Dips.

Rex was sad. He sat down.
CRUNCH!

Rex plodded off.

He felt bad.

Ted spotted Rex.

"Are you okay?" Ted said.

"No!" said Rex. "I have big feet, and short arms, and I cannot see."

"I can help," said Ted.

He took Rex into the wood.

They met Croc.

Croc put some little specs on Rex.

"Is this better?"

Rex looked. It was a blur.

"No," said Rex.

Croc put some big specs on Rex.

"Is this better?"

Rex looked. It was clear!

"Yes!" said Rex.

"I like my specs!" said Rex.

They were big and red.

"I can see!" he said.

Steg and Ted were playing.

"Can I play?" said Rex.

"Okay," said Steg.

Rex still had little hands.

And he still had big feet.

Rex!

But he was the best at hide and seek.

"I can see you all!"

Quiz

1. What sound did the ball make?
a) Crash!
b) Boom!
c) Pop!

2. What feet does Rex have?
a) Big
b) Small
c) Short

3. Who did Rex meet in the wood?
a) Dips
b) Croc
c) Steg

4. What helped Rex to see?

a) Little specs

b) Crazy specs

c) Big specs

5. What colour are Rex's specs?

a) Red

b) Blue

c) Green

Turn over for answers

Book Bands for Guided Reading

Pink
Red
Yellow
Blue
Green
Orange
Turquoise
Purple
Gold
White

The Institute of Education book banding system is a scale of colours that reflects the various levels of reading difficulty. The bands are assigned by taking into account the content, the language style, the layout and phonics. Word, phrase and sentence level work is also taken into consideration.

Maverick Early Readers are a bright, attractive range of books covering the pink to white bands. All of these books have been book banded for guided reading to the industry standard and edited by a leading educational consultant.

To view the whole Maverick Readers scheme, visit our website at
www.maverickearlyreaders.com

Or scan the QR code above to view our scheme instantly!

Quiz Answers: 1c, 2a, 3b, 4c, 5a